ANIMAL SURVIVAL

HUNTING TO SURVIVE

BY CLARA MacCARALD

CONTENT CONSULTANT
JESSE BALABAN-FELD, PhD
DEPARTMENT OF INTEGRATIVE BIOLOGY
OKLAHOMA STATE UNIVERSITY

Kids Core
An Imprint of Abdo Publishing
abdobooks.com

abdobooks.com

Published by Abdo Publishing, a division of ABDO, PO Box 398166, Minneapolis, Minnesota 55439. Copyright © 2023 by Abdo Consulting Group, Inc. International copyrights reserved in all countries. No part of this book may be reproduced in any form without written permission from the publisher. Kids Core™ is a trademark and logo of Abdo Publishing.

Printed in the United States of America, North Mankato, Minnesota.
052022
092022

THIS BOOK CONTAINS RECYCLED MATERIALS

Cover Photo: Martin Prochazkacz/Shutterstock Images
Interior Photos: Nico El Nino/Shutterstock Images, 4–5; Tory Kallman/Shutterstock Images, 7; PNQ Images/Shutterstock Images, 8, 28 (top); Lorraine Hudgins/Shutterstock Images, 9; J. Reineke/Shutterstock Images, 10; iStockphoto, 12–13; Fletcher & Baylis/Science Source, 14, 29 (top); Harry Collins Photography/Shutterstock Images, 17, 26; Danté Fenolio/Science Source, 18; Scott E. Read/Shutterstock Images, 20–21; Sergey Uryadnikov/Shutterstock Images, 23, 29 (bottom); Shutterstock Images, 25, 28 (bottom)

Editor: Ann Schwab
Series Designer: Katharine Hale

Library of Congress Control Number: 2021951726

Publisher's Cataloging-in-Publication Data

Names: MacCarald, Clara, author.
Title: Hunting to survive / by Clara MacCarald
Description: Minneapolis, Minnesota : Abdo Publishing, 2023 | Series: Animal survival | Includes online resources and index.
Identifiers: ISBN 9781532198526 (lib. bdg.) | ISBN 9781644947692 (pbk.) | ISBN 9781098272173 (ebook)
Subjects: LCSH: Animal defenses--Juvenile literature. | Defense measures--Juvenile literature. | Adaptation (Physiology)--Juvenile literature. | Animal behavior--Juvenile literature.
Classification: DDC 591.57--dc23

CONTENTS

A crabeater seal relaxes on an ice island, unaware of any predators nearby.

CHAPTER 1

MAKING WAVES

In the ocean near Antarctica, a group of hungry orcas spot a seal lying on a floating island of ice. The seal seems safe from the swimming predators. But the orcas have a trick to play.

First, the orcas pop their heads out of the water. They make sure the seal is the **species** they like to eat. The orcas gather. The animals know how to work as a team. They live and hunt together in family groups. Suddenly, all the orcas rush toward the ice, creating a wave.

Dolphin Smarts

Dolphins use lots of clever hunting techniques. Scientists noticed that some dolphins in Australia use sponges to hunt. A dolphin pulls a sea sponge from the sand. It fits the sponge over its beak like a glove. The dolphin uses its beak to hunt for fish in the sand. The sponge protects the beak from coral and rocks in the sand. This helps the dolphin find bottom-dwelling fish. These can have more nutrients than open-water fish.

Orcas pop their heads out of the water so they can see what's around them. This is called spy hopping.

At the last minute, they dive. Water washes over the ice. The wave sweeps the seal into the sea. The orcas move in for the kill.

Wolves are successful in catching prey less than 15 percent of the time.

Dragonflies hunt a variety of insects. This one is eating a damselfly.

Way of the Predator

A predator must catch animals to eat. A prey animal can survive only if it avoids predators. Prey animals have many **adaptations** to keep them safe, such as the spikes on a porcupine.

Hunting is not always easy. For example, wolves kill only about 14 of every 100 animals they go after. Some predators are more successful. Dragonflies catch nearly 95 percent of the prey they hunt.

Male lions, like the one pictured here, tend to hunt alone. But female lions hunt in groups.

Predators must have their own adaptations. They have sharp senses to help them find prey. Some lie in wait for a meal. Others go looking for their food. Predators may work alone or hunt in groups, like orcas do.

When a predator finds an animal to eat, it must catch it. Some animals use webs or **venom**. Others rely on speed. Hunters may use quick movements, sharp claws, and sharp teeth to make the kill. Making the kill means they will continue to survive.

Further Evidence

Look at the website below. Does it give any new evidence to support Chapter One?

Killer Whale Facts!

abdocorelibrary.com/hunting-to
-survive

As salmon pass through streams in the summer, brown bears are waiting to snatch them up. These bears can eat up to 100 pounds (45 kg) of salmon a day.

CHAPTER 2

LYING IN WAIT

Some predators **ambush** their prey. They may hide somewhere and watch. Or they may **lure** in their prey.

Setting the Trap

There are more than 100 species of trapdoor spiders worldwide.

A trapdoor spider creates a hidden tunnel to fool its prey.

Unlike many other spiders, trapdoor spiders don't build a web. These spiders dig a tunnel. They use their silk to build a door. They **camouflage** it with dirt and plants.

Trapdoor spiders hunt at night. A spider hides underneath a door waiting to ambush its prey. When an insect passes by, the spider dives out. It drags the prey inside. The spider uses venom to stop its meal from struggling.

Deadly Light

Female fireflies flash to males to signal they're ready to mate. But one kind of female firefly uses her light to hunt. She pretends to be a different firefly species when she signals. If a male of that species gets close enough, she eats him.

A Strike in the Night

Barred owls live in forests throughout North America. After sunset, a barred owl settles on a branch. It looks for rabbits, mice, or other tasty meals. Its large eyes see well in low light. A ring of feathers around its face funnels sound to its ears. Sometimes barred owls sit over water, watching for fish. When a prey animal moves, the owl dives. Its soft feathers cut silently through the air. The owl captures the prey in its claws. The owl will either swallow it whole or tear it into pieces before eating it.

A barred owl takes flight in search of prey.

A Fishing Fish

There are more than 200 species of anglerfish.
Most live deep in the ocean. They have huge
mouths and spiky teeth.

Anglerfish live in the deep ocean, at least 6,600 feet (2,000 m) below the surface.

The female lures in prey. A bone sticks out of her head like a fishing rod. Glowing flesh at the end acts as bait. When a fish comes near, the anglerfish strikes. An anglerfish can even swallow an animal twice her size. A male anglerfish doesn't hunt for food. Instead, he attaches himself to a female anglerfish. Their bodies merge, and he receives nutrients from her.

Deep-sea scientist Tracey Sutton helped discover a new species of anglerfish. He said:

> Every time we go out . . . there's a good chance we'll see something we've never seen before—the life at these depths is really amazing. . . . Our inventory of life in the vast ocean interior is far from complete.

Source: Joe Donzelli. "A New Deep-Sea Fish Species." *Nova Southeastern University Florida*, 5 Aug. 2015, nsunews.nova.edu. Accessed 3 Dec. 2021.

What's the Big Idea?

Read this quote carefully. What is its main idea? Explain how the main idea is supported by details.

A mountain lion uses speed
to pursue its prey.

CHAPTER 3

SEEKING PREY

Some predators seek out their prey. A predator may use its senses to find or track an animal. When the predator gets close, it might use a burst of speed to capture its meal.

Shark Attack!

Great white sharks are the world's largest predatory fish. They live in oceans all around the globe. Great whites hunt for fish, seals, whales, and more. They have amazing vision and hearing. And they can smell even a tiny bit of blood in the water.

When great whites find prey, they burst into speed. Some even leap out of the water.

Human Killers

Predators rarely kill humans, but it happens. Sharks killed 13 people in 2020. In India, tigers kill about 40 to 50 people a year. But the animal that kills the most humans is not a predator. Every year, mosquito bites lead to illnesses that kill 725,000 people.

Great white sharks are massive fish, weighing
4,000 to 7,000 pounds (1,800–3,200 kg).

They grab the animal with a giant bite. Great
whites don't chew their meals. Instead, they
swallow large pieces of the prey whole.

Surprised by Speed

Cheetahs are the world's fastest land animals. They live in Africa and Asia. Cheetahs use plants and mounds as cover when they hunt. When a cheetah gets close enough to its prey, the cat explodes into motion.

Cheetahs have light, flexible bodies built for speed. They can race up to 70 miles per hour (112 km/h). Once a cheetah catches its prey, it bites the animal's throat to stop it from breathing. Cheetahs catch half of the animals they chase. Of the animals they catch, they lose half to larger predators, such as lions and hyenas.

Cheetah Adaptations for Hunting

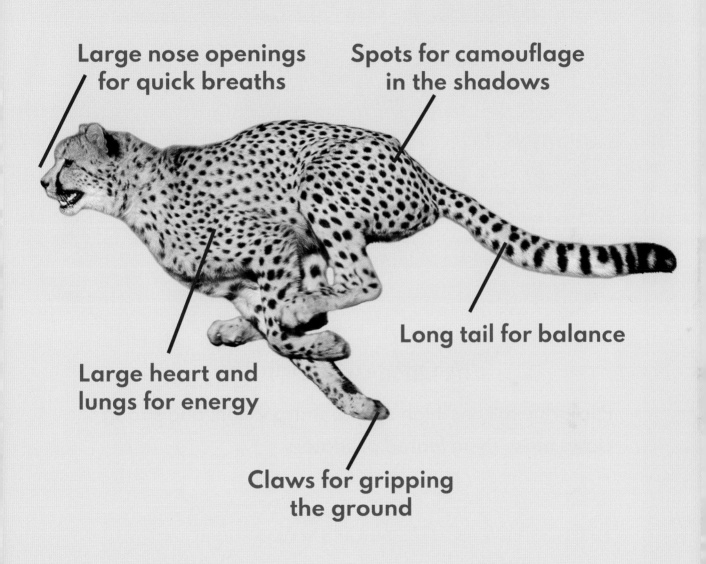

Large nose openings for quick breaths

Spots for camouflage in the shadows

Long tail for balance

Large heart and lungs for energy

Claws for gripping the ground

Cheetahs have a variety of adaptations that help them hunt.

Peregrine falcons' high speed, sharp vision, and strong claws make them feared predators.

Death from Above

Peregrine falcons are one of the fastest birds of prey. They live on six of the seven continents. Mostly, the falcons hunt other birds. Their prey can be as small as a hummingbird or larger than the falcons themselves.

Often a falcon hunts from high up in the sky. Its sharp eyes watch for birds below. When the falcon spots prey, it dives. It may reach speeds of 200 miles per hour (320 km/h). The falcon hits the other bird, knocking it to the ground. These falcons also have strong claws that can grab prey out of the air.

Explore Online

Visit the website below. Does it give any new information about birds of prey that wasn't in Chapter Three?

Birds of Prey

abdocorelibrary.com/hunting-to -survive

SURVIVAL FACTS

Predators must hunt and catch animals in order to eat.

Some predators use explosive speed to capture their prey.

Some predators have venom that stops their prey from struggling.

Adaptations such as a strong sense of smell help a predator find a meal.

Glossary

adaptations
features that a living thing has in order to help it survive

ambush
a surprise attack from a hiding place

camouflage
coloring or other features that help an animal or object look like its surroundings

lure
to draw another creature to a certain location, often by using bait

species
a group of similar living things that can have young together

venom
poison that an animal puts in another animal's body using teeth or a stinger

Online Resources

To learn more about hunting to survive, visit our free resource websites below.

Visit **abdocorelibrary.com** or scan this QR code for free Common Core resources for teachers and students, including vetted activities, multimedia, and booklinks, for deeper subject comprehension.

Visit **abdobooklinks.com** or scan this QR code for free additional online weblinks for further learning. These links are routinely monitored and updated to provide the most current information available.

Learn More

Harris, Tim. *How Spiders and Other Invertebrates Attack.* Wayland, 2022.

Olson, Elsie. *Animal Predator Smackdown.* Abdo, 2020.

Index

About the Author

Clara MacCarald is a freelance writer with a master's degree in ecology and natural resources. She lives with her family in an off-grid house nestled in the forests of central New York. When not parenting her daughter, she spends her time writing nonfiction books for kids.